The Laughing Postman Redelivers

True Stories by a Mail Carrier

Dee B. Myrick

*Dee B. Myrick
2016*

The Laughing Postman Redelivers

Dee B. Myrick email: thelaughingpostman@gmail.com

Cover credit: Dee B. Myrick

Editor: Conna Craig (connacraig@gmail.com)

Printed in the United States of America

Publisher: Classy Owl Publications

July 2016

ISBN-10: 1-945686-00-6
ISBN-13: 978-1-945686-00-9

TABLE OF CONTENTS

THE LAUGHING POSTMAN REDELIVERS

DEDICATION

This book is dedicated to Bridget.

BRIDGET

One of my favorite customers on my route was also a coworker. In fact she was the substitute for my route and it happened to be the route where she lived. She was smart and kind and had a contagious laugh.

During stormy days, she would find me on the route and insist on delivering part so I could "beat the storm" and finish work before the worst weather came. She loved to golf, so I repaid her by showing up the next time she worked the route and insisting on taking half so she could enjoy the beautiful day on the golf course. I never worried about my route or customers when I was on vacation or off sick when my friend carried the route for me.

I try to give plenty of notice when I need vacation or sick leave so I texted my friend the dates. She didn't answer. When I passed her house she was mowing the lawn, so I waved and she waved back. She would see the text later, I thought. Later that day, I remembered she hadn't texted me back so I sent another. The next day, still no answer so I stopped by her house and knocked.

Something wasn't right. Her cars were there but there was no answer to my knocks. The cat acted hungry and the plants hadn't been watered. Her inside dog, who was very old, was barking. He knew me and his bark wasn't the angry intruder alert but sounded sad and upset. He howled. I went next door but no one was home. I called my supervisor, who was also our friend, and told her my concern. She called the family contact on record.

I was almost finished with my route when I got the call. The family gave permission for the police to break in to the house. My friend was dead. She had a heart attack the day she had mowed her grass. She had medical problems but had never complained.

I think of my friend often. I still deliver that route and go by her house every day. She was a joy to know and work with. No matter how bad the day was, whatever the weather or mail volume, she always smiled and said, "One box at a time, we'll get this done."

I miss Bridget.

PART ONE. MAILBOXES

THE GREAT BILL ESCAPE

Part of my mail route was on a four-lane highway. Traffic was usually bad but on this day roadwork was making it horrendous. Cars would let me dodge in and out of the barely moving line. And to top it off it was a windy, blustery day.

I was reaching out with several pieces of mail to put in a mailbox when a gust of wind ripped the letters from my hand. I got out of my truck and picked up the mail up—except for one small, thin, postcard-sized letter.

The last letter acted like a miniature kite. Every time I thought I had it the darn thing would flitter away. Finally I managed to put my foot on it and pick it up.

When I turned back to my truck, someone beeped a horn in a congratulatory way. I realized I had been the momentary amusement for the stalled traffic.

There was nothing else I could do. I raised the

letters in a two-fisted winner's salute—and got lots
of happy horn blowing.

"CHEEKY" MAIL CARRIER

I delivered mail in a rural area that was in the process of becoming a high-end gated community. The streets were laid out in winding artistic loops with the purpose of having as much lakefront property as possible. This made for lots of dead end cul-de-sacs.

I discovered that bumping into the curbs to serve the boxes in these tight circles was destroying the sidewalls on my tires. This was expensive.

I asked the customers to move the problem boxes a few feet and all but one did. He told me in a nasal English accent that he liked his box where it was. I explained the situation regarding my tires but he just shrugged.

With my supervisor's permission, I curtailed delivery of his mail. This infuriated the man. He waylaid me and proceeded to rant, rave and cuss.

Exasperated, I told him, "Fine! You sit in your car on the passenger side, drive with your left foot and hand and if you can serve the box without running up the curb I will resume your mail delivery!"

He called my postmaster and claimed I had been rude and "cheeky." The postmaster told him my idea sounded good and he should try it.

Two days later the mailbox was moved. And my coworkers had a fine time calling me the "cheeky" carrier.

SUPERGLUED

Mailboxes come in many shapes and sizes. Customers would do themselves a favor if they would consult their mail carrier before buying a new one. Some boxes hold up better than others. Sometimes the fancy, expensive ones are the quickest to break down. And mailbox posts rot and get eaten by termites.

Sometimes mailboxes are victims. Several times in my postal career, I have seen the results of mailbox massacres. Usually this involves a truck, a baseball bat, Halloween or a football homecoming, beer, and stupid people. The physics of hitting a mailbox from a moving truck often results in personal injuries. Destroying mailboxes isn't just property damage; it's interfering with interstate commerce—which makes it a federal crime.

Mailbox vandalism isn't limited to smashing the boxes. Sometimes people will put what I think of as political statements in a mailbox. I've seen dead animals (including poisonous snakes posed to strike), broken eggs, underwear, and manure inside of mailboxes. One box was packed with rabbit poop. The owner was a local politician.

The worst case of vandalism I've seen involved a tiny tube. I approached a mailbox just as I do hundreds of times a day. I pulled up, mail in hand and reached up to pull the lid. It didn't open. Sometimes box hinges get rusty, sometimes lids swell in the heat, or ice closed in the cold, and sometimes the owners push the doors extra hard and they stick. I pulled harder. Nothing. I put the truck in park and used both hands. The lid refused to budge.

So I put the mail in the "return to office" pile and went to the next box. Same thing, couldn't open it. I went to the next boxes in that neighborhood and couldn't open nearly twenty of them. At the last box, my question about what had gone on was answered. On the ground by the last unopenable mailbox was a tiny tube of... superglue.

The parents of three 12-year-old boys had to replace their neighbors' mailboxes.

Duct Taped

Providing a proper mail receptacle is the responsibility of the customer. Whether to accept that mailbox is up to the carrier. Most mailboxes are purchased from a store but some are handmade. If they are watertight and safe to open and close, I'm o.k. with them. Once the carrier places mail in a box, that mailbox is considered approved. To stop delivery after that requires an act of the postmaster or a supervisor.

One household on my route had its mailbox crushed, most likely by an eighteen-wheeler cutting the curve too sharp. I took the mail to the house to let them know about the demise of their mailbox. They told me it would be replaced soon. The next day, a cheap plastic mailbox was loosely nailed to a post. Inside was a note saying that a better mailbox would be up by the weekend. So I delivered.

Several weekends later, the box had not been improved. Instead, the nails holding the box to the post had worked loose and the mailbox fell off when I shut the lid. I left a nice note asking the customer to please secure the mailbox to the post. The next day I stopped several feet before the box. I couldn't believe what I was seeing.

Someone had used an entire industrial-sized roll of duct tape on the mailbox to hold it to the post. Starting about halfway up the post and wrapping over the middle of the box, the shining silver tape engulfed the mailbox. Even the flag had a star-shaped duct tape cover.

I laughed and put the mail in the box.

PART TWO. POSTAL EQUIPMENT

B.C. (Before Cell Phones)

When cell phones first came out they were large, bulky things that came in a lunch-box sized bag. I had a friend working for the new mobile phone company and she asked me to give her business card to my coworkers.

My fellow carriers and I decided the newfangled phone was just some gadget or fad that would soon pass. One of the old-timers laughed at me and threw his card in the garbage.

The next week, that old-timer witnessed a motorcycle wreck and saved a young man's life by applying a tourniquet. The carrier told me he would have given anything for that bag phone in those bloody long moments before help arrived.

Within a few weeks, every rural carrier in my office owned one of those "bag phones."

THE LAUGHING POSTMAN REDELIVERS

SHARPEST SCISSORS

Over the years, the duties of a rural letter carrier have increased. One of those is breaking down the mail. "Flats" are magazines, legal-sized envelopes and other mail larger than standard letters. This type of mail can come in bundles that are wrapped in plastic, tied with strings or fastened with hard plastic cords. All have to be cut and removed before we can start putting the mail in route order.

The postal service, in its wisdom, provided us with a ring knife. It wasn't really a ring. Or a knife. It was a large metal loop that fit loosely over the index finger and had a curved blade we were supposed to use to cut plastic and strings. The little blade was never sharp and did not work very well.

Most of us carriers brought our own scissors to use, and we kept them in the drawers under our worktable. Over time, these scissors would lose their sharpness and we would trade them for new ones. George was an older carrier and one day he offered to take our scissors home with him and sharpen them. I wasn't working that day so I wasn't aware that my dull scissors had been transformed into lethal weapons.

So it was that I promptly cut myself with my newly sharpened scissors. And I wasn't the only one. Several carriers, used to having to put considerable pressure on the scissors to cut the plastic, managed to cut themselves also. The next time George offered to sharpen scissors we all yelled, "No!" In chorus.

Scanner Scares

One of the advantages of being rural letter carriers over city carriers is that we work on salary instead of hourly. City carriers get paid by the hour so their supervisors are always pushing them to hurry, hurry. Rural carriers get paid the same even if we take longer on some days so the supervisors leave us alone. Until recently.

Technology is changing the way the postal service works. When I started, we would hand-write forwarding addresses and now computers do it automatically with bar codes. Clerks would sort the mail to routes and now huge machines do it, replacing almost an entire shift of postal workers. We got written signatures on little slips of paper for proof of delivery for accountable mail. Now the customer signs a small hand-held computer called a "scanner" and the signature is almost instantly uploaded to the Internet.

This scanner is a pain. I understand it is

necessary for the postal service to keep up with our competition. But it is awkward to handle and sometimes refuses to read a bar code. Then we have to punch in the long numerical code by hand. And sometimes the darn things talk to us.

The first time my scanner spoke I almost ran off the road. As far as I was concerned, I was alone in the world, moseying along to my next mailbox when a deep male voice spoke from the empty seat next to me.

I jerked my head to look and also jerked the steering wheel. Luckily no other cars were on the road at that time. I didn't understand what it said and it was not repeated. When I returned to the post office and told my supervisor, he laughed.

The scanner voice option was supposed to start the next week and we were going to have a service talk explaining the new procedures.

GAS CANS AND WATERMELONS

One of my customers lived beside a busy highway. I was delivering a parcel to his garage door when I noticed a handwritten sign leaning against several gas cans.

The sign read, "One of these Gas Cans Has Sugar Added." I asked him why he did that. Sugar destroys engines, he explained. People had been stealing his gas, but not after he put up the sign.

My grandfather had been a rural letter carrier. He told me about a customer of his who had grown several acres of watermelons. Thieves were sneaking in late at night and stealing the watermelons. My grandfather's customer put up a sign.

"One of these Watermelons Is Poisoned!"

A couple of days later, someone had added to the sign. They had crossed out the word "one" and replaced it. Now the sign read:

"Two of these Watermelons Is Poisoned!"

MUFFLER TEST

I had a request for a redelivery of a parcel for a customer who lived at the end of a really bad road. When I delivered her parcel, she was angry that the substitute had left her a notice the day before instead of delivering it. "Was he lazy?" she asked me.

"Nope," I told her, "It was the muffler test."

I explained.

Most rural mail routes are delivered in personally owned vehicles. We are not required to put our vehicles at risk on roads with deep potholes, ruts, unsafe bridges, or across cattle gaps. One carrier explained to me early in my career that the true test to decide to use a road was whether or not your car's muffler might be scraped off.

"I have a truck," I told her, "that can go over the ruts in your road. The sub has a small car. If he had come up your road he would have lost his muffler."

"Oh," she said, her anger gone. "I guess I should

fix my road."

"Yep," was my reply.

LOUD RADIO

Traveling rural roads with the window down makes it hard to hear the radio. So maybe, I have my radio turned up a little high. A tiny bit. Maybe. One of my customers told me she could hear me coming a half-mile away. That's how she knew to leave her porch swing and meet me at the mailbox even before I rounded the curve and came into sight.

I was listening to oldies and really enjoying the day's selection when I saw my customer standing by her mailbox. As I slowed down, I could see she was holding her side. Then I saw she was laughing. Laughing very hard.

I lifted my chin with dignity and handed her the mail without saying a word. It wasn't *that* funny, I thought.

The song was "Please Mr. Postman" by the Marvelettes.

FROGGER

I was a child when video games were invented. The first one I remember shot BBs at pop-up figures in a tiny Western town. It cost a nickel. Then there were pinball machines. I had to stand in a chair to play those, and I got two games for a quarter. And then there was Pong, the tennis-like game that could hook up to any TV and consisted of two white lines and a white dot. It was actually pretty fun and my brother and I played for hours.

The game that addicted me was Frogger. It was more advanced and the goal was to move the frog across the river by jumping on logs without it falling in or getting eaten by alligators and turtles. It required timing and judgment on speeds of the logs and the ability of the frog to jump. I spent hours and hours playing this silly game. My mom thought I was wasting my time. Looking back, I would agree—except for one thing.

Years later, I'm all grown up and running a

rural mail route. This route had highways as well as county roads and a major landfill. And so it was that I found myself following a truck full of used tires on the highway. We were at the top speed limit when I saw the truck hit a bump in the road and the top tire fall out. And watched it bounce in front of me.

I judged the height of the first bounce and the speed we were traveling and made a quick decision. I tapped my brakes at just the right moment and the tire bounced over the hood of my small Nissan car and off the road. In my rear view mirror, I watched the tire roll down the embankment.

So all those hours on the video game hadn't been wasted after all.

REAR VIEW MIRRORS

My dad worked for the United States Post Office for twenty-four years. He had retired from the Marine Corps with twenty years and gone to college on the GI bill. After taking the postal exam (he scored in the upper 90s) he got work as a clerk/carrier. My dad worked as a clerk, supervisor, temporary postmaster (officer in charge) and finally as a rural carrier in a very small town. He liked the last job the best.

He told me this story. His mail route was over a hundred miles long with lots of washed out gravel roads and one-lane roads. He had only a few hundred mail customers because most of his route was National Forest. And it was a log truck, he told me, that almost killed him.

Rear view mirrors are a wonderful invention. We mail carriers depend on all three mirrors for pulling in and out of traffic as we serve our mailboxes. My dad was serving a mailbox at the bottom of a hill when he looked in the rear view mirror and saw a fully loaded log truck topping the hill. In the oncoming traffic was a van. Thinking quickly, my dad punched the accelerator and went in the ditch. The truck managed to stop further down the road and the driver walked back to help my dad get his car out of the ditch. The van kept going.

"I'm really glad you got out of the way," the driver told my dad. "I knew I couldn't stop. Figured the van might have kids so I decided if I had to hit someone it was going to be you."

I hope that whoever invented rear view mirrors is very rich.

PART THREE. SPECIAL DELIVERIES

TARRED AND FEATHERED

My grandfather was a rural carrier. In the latter years of his life after he was long retired and I was just beginning my career, we would compare stories of postal life.

In his time, people would mail order almost anything. While I have delivered baby chicks in boxes on a regular basis, he would have full-grown chickens in slated crates. And if it was a cold day he would keep them in the cab of his truck.

Pawpaw also had to apply glue to stamps to make them stick to letters and he had a small scale to determine weight. The glue was in a jar with a dabber attached to the lid.

One cold spring, day he had two full-grown roosters in one wire crate to deliver. Yes, two roosters, one cage. They fought and feathers flew.

He was driving a bumpy gravel road and his glue jar bounced opened. Glue spilled. Everywhere. It got on him, all over the inside of his truck and on the mail.

Feathers and glue. While driving with the window down.

DINOSAURS

The United States Postal Service sells stamps as proof of purchase for the service of transporting mail from one place to another. Stamps are NOT taxes and the post office doesn't use any federal tax money to stay in business. Before 1840, customers paid for their mail when they received it. People would cheat by putting secret codes on the outside of the envelope and then the receiving customer would refuse to pay. So the British began charging the mail sender up front and made the first stamp. America soon followed and made two stamps, one with Benjamin Franklin for five cents and one with George Washington for 10 cents. The five-cent stamp paid for letters being delivered less than 300 miles and the 10-cent stamp for letters mailed between 300 and 3,000 miles.

I've had many interesting experiences involving stamps during the 30-plus years I've worked for the postal service. But the one about the dinosaurs still makes me smile. An elderly customer on my route requested that I please get for her the largest stamps available because her arthritis made it difficult to hold them. So when she ordered stamps, I would go to the clerk and we would go through the stacks of sheet stamps, instead of the smaller books, and pick out the biggest ones.

The largest stamps at that time were dinosaur stamps. The lady looked at me funny and said she didn't believe in dinosaurs. After a moment's thought she decided she would accept them, but said that she would use a different stamp to mail in her church tithe.

DO NOT BEND

"Do Not Bend" mail is usually a magazine-sized envelope that the sender writes on or on which the user has stamped the words "Do Not Bend." The postal service treats these as fragile parcels. I had a photography business for a few years and had some issues with photos arriving creased and bent. This ruined them. So when I became a rural letter carrier, I was very careful with this type of mail.

One of my favorite customers was eagerly waiting for wedding photos of her niece. When they came I placed the thin Do Not Bend envelope between two larger ridged parcels to protect them. Then when I shifted mail for the next part of my route, I was extra careful that nothing smashed the fragile photos.

It was with relief that I made it to the photos' address and could hand over the Do Not Bend to its owner. I beeped the horn to let my customer know I was coming. I went up to the house with all the lady's mail to save her a trip to the mailbox. Her teenaged granddaughter answered the door and before I could open my mouth grabbed the mail and folded the Do Not Envelope around the other mail. And squeezed. I heard the crunch as the photo cracked.

C.O.D.

"C.O.D." means cash on delivery mail. This is when a customer purchases something and payment is made to the mail carrier at the time of delivery, and then the post office sends the money to the sender. This was a lot more common a long time ago. My grandfather was a rural carrier substitute for 17 years (he chose to not go full-time). He told me that people bought a lot of things this way: school supplies, clothes, medicines, and much more. Now we have credit and debit cards and order things online. When a carrier has a C.O.D. to deliver, we are issued the mail by a clerk who signs the item out to us. In the afternoon we either bring the C.O.D. mail back or the money. If there's no money or mail, we have to pay out of our own pocket.

My grandfather told me this story. He had a C.O.D. parcel, a tube that was for a couple of hundred dollars. Pawpaw got out of his truck and the man met him in the yard. The man wanted to open the parcel before paying for it. My grandfather said no, it had to be bought first. The man grabbed the parcel from pawpaw and ran.

Knowing that if he didn't get the parcel back he would have to pay for it himself, my grandfather ran after the man and, catching up, he tackled the customer. Pawpaw snatched the tube back and for good measure he whopped the customer on the head with it a few times.

Then he asked if the man wanted to pay for the parcel or not. The man did. What made my grandfather really mad was that when the man opened his wallet to pay, it was full of $100 bills.

And what was the customer thinking? The post office knew where he lived!

DAYS OF OUR LIVES

Customers will call in complaints for just about anything. Hitting mailboxes (the paint streak on the box was blue and my truck was brown), mis-boxed mail (sometimes true but mostly not), denting garbage cans (never, I refuse to get that close to the smelly things) and not attempting parcels or mail that requires a signature.

Unless there is a dangerous dog, I *always* go to the door to try to deliver special delivery items of mail. One day, I had made just such an attempt. When I returned to the post office that afternoon, my supervisor accused me of skipping the delivery. The customer had gone to the mailbox and found the notice slip. She had been home all day and claimed I hadn't knocked or rung the doorbell.

I had rung the doorbell and knocked several times to get the customer's attention, I explained to my boss. But the TV was so loud she couldn't hear me. "Prove it," my frowning supervisor said. Well

I did.

"Days of our Lives was on and Bo and Hope were arguing about Bo's motorcycle."

And yes I know this dates me. Again.

SPOILED FISH

I am an optimistic person. I'm also trusting and naïve. So when a customer received an overnight parcel from Mexico that stank to high heaven, I was worried that something had spoiled. The customer just smiled, said "No problem," and happily signed for the parcel.

And a few weeks later, he got another spoiled smelly parcel. Whatever he was ordering wasn't getting to him fast enough, I thought, and felt bad because our overnight express service had failed.

When the next rotten parcel arrived, it came with a Postal Inspector. The spoiled fish, he explained to me, was to hide the smell of cocaine from the drug dogs. He delivered the parcel and arrested the man.

DOG EATS PARCEL

Making decisions about parcel deliveries is time consuming, especially on a new route. We are responsible for the mail until it is in the mailbox and the lid is shut. After that it belongs to the customer. So if a parcel fits in the mailbox (we *love* big mailboxes) nothing else has to be done.

But if the parcel doesn't fit, then the decision-making cranks up a notch. Does the customer want the parcel left or returned to the post office for pick-up? Do they have a dog that will bite me or shred the parcel? Front door or back door?

I thought a particular address was easy, because the customer had given permission in writing to have parcels left at the house and had specified the back door. Yea!

The next morning, the customer called to complain that the parcel had been chewed by a dog. My supervisor said I had to pay for the parcel or be fired.

"They don't have a dog," I told him. He just shrugged. I was a sub at the time and didn't know my rights.

When I got to the house with the chewed-on parcel the lady saw me digging for change to pay for the parcel. She was surprised that I was the one who had to pay. She thought some mysterious postal fund would supply the money. She also thought that she would get the money and get to keep the parcel. Nope I told her, we buy it we own it. You use the money to purchase another one.

She was sorry, she told me, to cause trouble. She showed me the parcel and only a small corner had been chewed. The book wasn't even damaged. I kept my money and she kept the book. In the future, I put the parcels out of reach of the neighbors' dogs.

PARCEL RETURNS

The invention of the home shopping TV shows changed the world. In my grandfather's time, the Sears and J.C. Penney catalogs were a big deal. The mailman would deliver the thick, heavy catalogs to almost everyone on a mail route. Then the carrier would pick up the order envelopes and, a few weeks later, deliver the merchandise.

Eventually stores opened in almost every town and customers went to malls to buy things. Next came the TV shopping channels. And the post office was back in the parcel business again.

I have a few customers who dearly love to buy things they see on TV. They get caught up in the auctions, they tell me, and get a rush from snatching a deal before the item runs out. Some of my customers with physical limitations do most of their shopping this way. About a third of my daily parcels are for these customers.

One of my regular deliveries goes to a mother

and grown son. They get dozens of parcels every week. And about once a month, I get a note in the box to come to the house for a pick up. They return 80 percent of the parcels. The son told me his mother was addicted to the shopping shows.

The next time I went for a pick-up, the mother told me *her son* was addicted to the shopping shows.

PART FOUR. POSTAL LIFE

CANDID CAMERA

Story by L. Haley

I thought I had found the perfect spot on one of the mail routes to stop and pee. Not too much of a choice available sometimes. I've used this little hidden spot three or four times now. I even told another carrier, Kristy, about it so she could take advantage while she was out there.

Kristy called to tell me today—after she already went—that she saw a sign posted that says, "Smile, you're on camera."

DIVINITY DEPRIVED

There comes a time in a mail carrier's career when she chooses to change routes. This can be a difficult decision for lots of reasons. Changing routes means having to learn new roads, mailboxes, potholes, dog hazards, and customers. And one of the sad results is leaving customers who have become friends.

For more than 12 years, I ran a mail route that I dearly loved. By giving good service and the luck of having several businesses that received and sent a lot of mail build on my route, my salary was at the upper range and very comfortable. My husband's family lived on the route and the church we married in was located there. In fact, the church had named a new building after my granny-in-law.

Then the postal service chose to cut my route by taking part of it to make another route. At around the same time, several of my high-volume businesses either moved or closed. I knew that my nice salary was ruined and when the opportunity came, I changed to a new route that would pay more. This was a hard decision because of the divinity.

One of my most favorite foods of all time is divinity candy. It is made from egg whites, corn syrup, chopped pecans and sugar. Lots of sugar. Humidity affects the making of this candy so it takes skill and practice to get it right. The candy might be too dry or worse, too gooey, if everything doesn't go just right. Mrs. S was an angel at making divinity candy and once she knew how much I liked it, she would often leave me some in the mailbox. Whenever her flag was up, I would start to salivate like Pavlov's dog.

So it was with total disbelief when I heard from relatives that the carrier who took the route after me had treated Mrs. S rudely. First, she was an older lady and I was raised to respect my elders. Second, over a hundred customers on that route were her relatives or her direct descendants.

That idiot carrier. I felt anger that a coworker

would treat my former customer badly. Then
I pitied him. He would never, ever get any of that
divine divinity.

P. O. SHORTS

A mail carrier knows he or she is running late at the end of October when the customer answers the door for a parcel and says, "Great costume!" and offers some candy.

One way to tell a rural letter carrier is her right arm is much more tanned than her left arm. The right arm goes out the car window to put mail in the mailboxes.

Never buy a used vehicle that has lots of little scratches on the passenger side door. These are caused by mailbox lids dropping on the side of the vehicle when we put mail in the box. The miles on the speedometer do not accurately reflect the wear and tear that our start-and-stop mail routes require.

Never, ever eat the food gifts from a customer who is a hoarder.

Cowboy Way

Periodically, post office management "inspects" our rural routes. Usually this means they ride with us on the route for the day and check that the paperwork is correct. This is time-consuming for the supervisors and slows the carriers down, so sometimes they have the subs come in and run part of the route while we ride with the supervisors without the mail.

One time I had the joy of not one but two supervisors inspecting my route, double-checking the street names, directions and that the mailboxes existed. The day started with the two grown men arguing over whose personal truck they would use, where they would get something to eat and who had to do the paperwork. I was completely ignored until we reached the parking lot.

Then I informed them that I was going to sit in the middle of the truck because I didn't want to drive or get out to open the gates. This silenced the men, but only for a moment. "What gates?" they asked, flipping through the pages of my route description.

I just smiled and got in the truck.

9/11: A MAIL CARRIER'S STORY

I was casing mail in preparation for delivering my route on September 11, 2001, and listening to a local radio station on headphones when the DJ broke in and reported the plane crash in New York. They thought it was an accident.

The next hours revealed the truth. We as a nation had been attacked and thousands of people had been murdered.

We all remember emotions of that day. Shock, anger, fear, compassion for the victims, and a desperate need for information. I know I delivered mail that day but I don't remember much about it.

The next day, I picked up more misdelivered mail and mistakes from that one day than I think I made in all my years of service combined. And received not one complaint from my customers.

IF I DIED

If I died before I retire, this is what I think my coworkers would say about me.

The postmaster. "Well, she was working here before I came and I thought she'd be here after I left." (I actually told a postmaster that once and it was true.)

The supervisors. "She doesn't take off work just because it's a hard day and she goes easy on the subs." (A sub told me that a supervisor said this.)

The clerks. "She doesn't fuss when the trucks come late or when we bring last-minute extra mail."

City carriers. "Didn't really know her; she worked on the other end of the building. She always helped with the food drive even though she didn't get paid for it."

The customers. "We're gonna miss her. She was hardly ever late and would check on momma for us. Always said 'Sir' and 'Ma'am.'"

My fellow rural carriers. "Dang, we're gonna miss those egg salad sandwiches! When you think they will post her route?"

DON'T BARK

I had to have a minor outpatient surgery recently and I was a little nervous. The nurses were bustling about and one was tying my arms to the little boards He asked me if I knew one of my arms had a deeper tan than the other.

I am a rural mail carrier. I sit on the passenger side of the vehicle and put mail out the window with my right arm. That arm gets more sun than the other and hence the darker tan. I answered the nurse that yes I knew my right arm was darker tanned than my left. It was an occupational hazard.

The nurse had already given me some happy juice and I was staring up, thinking that the hospital should put some pretty pictures on the ceiling. Butterflies. Yes, butterfly pictures would be nice.

And puppies, I thought. There should be butterflies and puppies on the ceiling. The nurse asked me, "What do you do?"

"I'm a mail carrier," I told him. The edges of my

vision were getting blurry.

Another nurse behind me said the inevitable. "Let's hope you don't 'go postal' on us, ha ha."

Kittens should also be on the ceiling, I thought. Butterflies, puppies, and kittens. My vision was going from blurry to shadows as I heard myself say, "Nobody bark like a dog and I promise to stay on the surgical table."

Laughter followed me as I faded out.

Senior in the Craft

I was very young when I was hired by the U. S. Postal Service. Everyone in the rural craft was older than me by decades. They called me the "baby duck," and I was never sure if it was intended in a friendly way or not. It was a part-time job and I was a college student, unsure what I wanted to do for a career. I found that I really enjoyed working outside and 30-plus years later, I'm still employed by the postal service.

An older man worked next to me for the office part of our day. Mr. L informed me on my third day of work that he was senior in the craft and I should remember that. I had no clue what he meant so I just said, "Yes, sir!"

The rural craft had thirteen routes at that time and worked out of the basement of the old post office. In our workspace, we had two garbage cans. These two cans sat at two routes next to each other and everyone else had to leave their work area and walk across the room to use the cans. Lucky me, I worked closer to one than the other so I didn't have as far to go. I mentioned to Mr. L that it would be fair if the garbage cans were centrally located.

He frowned and looked over his glasses at me. "That's MY can and I. Am. Senior. In. The. Craft."

Same thing happened with the fans. Some routes were allowed to have them, some not. Years later, a new post office was built and all routes got our own garbage cans. Not fans though—they took too much electricity.

Over the years, equipment we used at the post office changed. Some changes were improvements, some not. The hampers (I called them "buggies") that we first used to transport the mail from the post office to our vehicles were originally small canvas bags on wheels. It would take multiple trips do the job. Then management got smart and got the larger size buggies and we eliminated the extra trips, at least on normal mail-volume days.

I really liked the bigger buggy. It basically was a wooden pallet on wheels with a wire frame and a sturdy, thick canvas that could hold lots of mail and parcels. Bungee cords held the cloth sides up and, as we filled the buggy, it would settle down. As we emptied them, they would lift back up so shorter people like me didn't fall in headfirst. The wheels rolled well and I could easily push it across our bumpy brick-paved parking lot.

Then the post office started replacing the lightweight canvas buggies with heavier but smaller plastic ones. No bungee cords and two of the four wheels didn't swivel so it was hard to turn the thing. I asked management to *not* replace my buggy. They agreed with the understanding that when it broke, I'd be getting the plastic one.

Years later, I still have same buggy. A new guy was having issues with his plastic buggy. It wouldn't turn at the bottom of the ramp and the volume of his route meant he had to make multiple trips to load his truck. He stomped angrily over to my work area and demanded to know why I was so special that I got to have the canvas buggy.

Until that moment, I hadn't thought of Mr. L in

years.

I looked over my glasses at the newbie and informed him that I. Am. Senior. In. The. Craft.

PART FIVE. CRITTERS

JUST BIRDS

The standard cliché about the mailman is that dogs hate us. This is simply not true. When dogs see the same person day after day, they stop treating that person like a stranger. When the dog's owner tells the dog to be quiet and is nice to the mail carrier, the dog understands that we are not strangers. In thirty-plus years of delivering mail I've been bitten only once. By a Chihuahua. It was a bad bite and because it partially severed a tendon it took months to heal.

I have been attacked by other animals. I drove up a long driveway to a beautiful house by a lake. The dogs were friendly so I didn't hesitate to get out with the parcel. Three happy dogs danced around me as I headed for the door.

I heard the geese before I saw them. They came around the house in a tight formation of large dingy white bodies and snake-like necks, honking and screeching. The dogs abandoned me, racing away.

I thought, "It's only birds, what's the big deal?"
Then the birds attacked. Before I managed to retreat
back to my truck, I was beaten with wings and
stabbed with blunt beaks.

I had scratches from the wings and deep bruises
from the beaks. I never underestimated "just birds"
again.

ABOVE AND BEYOND

I love the dogs on my route. Dogs are individuals, just like people. They can be grumpy, happy, sad, moody or funny. I have found lost dogs and delivered them home. I give treats (with the owner's permission). I've spread the news about free puppies. I love dogs. And I'm not the only mail carrier who feels this way.

Early one morning, I was walking into the post office to start my day when I noticed a city carrier walking with a sack of dog food slung over his shoulder. That's unusual, I thought. He saw the look on my face and laughed.

He explained that his customers had gone on vacation and asked him to check on their dogs. The customers were delayed in getting home, and the automatic dog feeder had run out. He was going to fill it up.

Now *that's* going above and beyond.

RESCUING TURTLES

Some rural routes are very... rural. They can be over a hundred miles long but have few mailboxes. My grandfather and my dad had routes like that. I work in a more populated area so the routes I've delivered have fewer miles and lots more mailboxes.

One of my favorite routes was a mixture. The first part of the route consisted of businesses and apartments. I delivered over two-thirds of my daily volume of mail in a short period of time. Then I reached the real "rural" part and traveled miles between mailboxes. On some side roads, I would not meet any other cars for weeks at a time.

It was on one of these side roads I rescued the box turtle. I traveled four miles into the country on a narrow road and then back out to the main road after serving only a handful of mailboxes. In more than six months, I had met only three other vehicles, all on separate occasions.

On the way in, I noticed a small box turtle upside down on the road. It was stretching its neck out, twisting, and its little legs were making swimming motions. I decided that I would rescue the turtle on my way back if it hadn't managed to flip itself over. It hadn't, so I stopped in the road, put my truck in park, turned off the engine and got out.

At this time in my career I had a distinctive truck. Toyotas were the truck of preference for rural mail carriers because they were sturdy and voted most likely to be paid for before the transmission went out. When I went to buy mine, the dealer didn't have many options. I wanted a green one. The one they had wasn't green so the salesman dropped the price. Substantially. And then again. Long story short, I got the truck cheap and the Toyota dealership offered me a job. "Midnight blue" isn't blue. It's purple. My mail customers, my children, my hometown, coworkers and my children's friends all know who drives the purple truck. Add a flashing white light on the top, hazard lights blinking, me sitting in the passenger seat and *nobody* in the driver's side, and my truck gets remembered.

So I had just reached down to pick up the small turtle when I heard a truck coming. And then another one from the other direction. As kismet happens, the two trucks met in the middle with me standing in the road holding a turtle.

The first old guy yells—not to me but to the other old guy—"What's going on?"

Second guy yells back, " It's the mail lady! Is she broke down?"

First guy: "I don't think so, maybe she's got a flat?"

Second guy: "Nope, they all look good to me!"

My head is bouncing back and forth as if I were at a tennis match.

First guy finally asks, " Well girl, what are you doing?"

I haven't been a girl for a few decades at this point but I answered politely, "Rescuing this turtle." I held up the turtle as proof.

Said turtle decides this is the perfect time for a potty break and releases a smelly liquid stream. Three people make no sound as this small animal pees and pees and pees. The volume was remarkable.

First guy stares at me and slowly drives by. Second guy drives by, also staring. Neither made another comment.

I released the turtle in the grass. I hope it was on the side of the road it had been traveling toward.

GOD'S CUTEST CREATIONS

I love the people on my mail route. I have the nicest, most thoughtful customers. They pray for me in bad weather and offer sanctuary in their homes. They give me cold drinks in the heat of summer and warm banana nut bread in the cold of winter. I receive waves and smiles, sweet treats and thankful notes. I love my customers.

I also love the animals on my route. Contrary to postal myth, most dogs know their mail carrier and are polite, even friendly. I look forward to seeing them and mourn when they pass. I love seeing the newborn calves and horses and watching them grow. Sometimes birds build nests by or in mailboxes and I get glimpses as the eggs hatch and the baby birds grow into adults.

We recently received new scanners for work. The scanners are for reading barcodes and recording proof of delivery. These new and improved devices are supposed to make life easier.

They do read the barcodes quickly and have more options to explain why delivery couldn't happen. They also talk to us (first time scared me and almost made me run off the road) and tell management where we are.

Rumor is that the scanners can listen in on us and tell management how long we stay in one place. I'm not sure about the first part of the rumor, but I do know that other carriers have been warned by management about spending too much time at one location.

I have a long, narrow road with a few houses at the end where I sometimes take a short break. The trees line the road and provide beautiful shade with a few sunbeams sprinkling through. After the new scanners came, I felt that I shouldn't take that break. One day I saw a tiny furry critter in the road so I slowed. It was a chipmunk playing in the fallen leaves and the sunlight.

That tiny fuzzy animal was no bigger than my hand. It was zigzagging in the sunbeams, in, out, over and under the leaves. Almost-red fur with thin

white stripes down its back and a short tail…
I believe it was one of the cutest things I've ever
seen. Another one came onto the road and played in
the leaves. And another one.

I thought briefly about my tattletale scanner and
the possible discipline for spending to much time
between mailboxes. To heck with the dang scanner.
I reached over and turned off my truck engine.
There were now five chipmunks playing in the sun-
dappled, leaf-covered road.

I felt blessed to witness the joy of some of God's
cutest creations.

PART SIX. CUSTOMERS

SINGING IN THE RAIN

Sometimes letter carriers are in a world of our own. On some routes I've worked, most of the customers were not home during the week and I could work for hours without seeing a person. Dogs, yes, but no customers. Just me and the mailboxes.

On one memorable rainy day I was serving a row of twelve boxes. I had my favorite radio station on and it was playing oldies from my high school days. I was happily singing along with the Eagles when I heard someone clear his throat.

Embarrassed, I stopped singing and looked at the customer, holding his an umbrella and waiting for his mail.

"Can I help you, sir?" I asked.

"Yes," he replied, smiling. "Don't quit your day job."

COUNTING CHILDREN

When I first started working for the postal service as a rural carrier substitute, summers were a time when children played outdoors. We carriers had safety meetings about watching for children in the streets. Posters advised us to be cautious and alert about children. All summer kids would be riding bikes, roller skating, or just playing games in the yards and roads.

Now I can go a whole week without seeing any children outside anytime—summer, winter, fall, or spring. I know they live on my route. I saw the pink or blue ribbon on the mailbox when they came home from the hospital. I see the birthday parcels from grandparents, and the balloons tied to the mailbox. Every summer the school sends out the final grades at the end of the year. I guess the children are inside watching TV and playing video games.

In the old days, kids played outside. I had a

method of keeping track of the children as I served mailboxes in a subdivision where the boxes are close together. I would count all the children I could see. One, two, three, until they were all counted. Then, after placing mail in a mailbox and before taking my foot off the brake, I would count them again. Counting children prevented horrible accidents on several occasions.

This is the incident that started me counting kids. Three young boys were walking across yards on my right, carrying basketballs and being followed by a much younger and shorter little sister. The boys were obviously ignoring her and she had to trot to keep up. I served the next mailbox and started to let off the brake when I noticed the boys had crossed the road to my left. The little sister had disappeared. Then she reappeared. From right in front of my truck.

When I see children on my route I count them— both before *and* after I put mail in a mailbox and drive away.

AND THE BLIND STILL DRIVE

I knew an elderly man on my route who would sit in the shade of an old oak tree to wait for the mail. When I served his mailbox, we would visit some. Over the years, his eyesight began to fail. He tried cataract surgery but, in his words, "It didn't take." He started getting books on tape labeled "For the blind."

So it was with surprise I saw the old man driving toward me on a country back road. His ancient truck was weaving in and out of my lane, so I drove down a driveway and let him have the entire road. Then I turned around and followed him to the little store.

He ran out of tobacco, he told me. I chastised him about nearly running into me and pointed out that children on bicycles often used that road. He promised he wouldn't drive anymore. I followed him home to make sure he got there.

Several months later, I looked up from a

mailbox to see the ancient truck again weaving toward me. This time the old man was in the passenger seat. At first I didn't see anyone driving, but then a small head popped up to peak over the steering wheel. Again, I turned around and followed the old truck to the country store.

They needed milk, the legally blind old man said, and since he had promised not to drive he had his 10-year-old grandson drive instead. The boy grinned and told me he drove all the time, but only to the store.

Ain't Y'all Found Me Yet?

Before my dad became a rural letter carrier, he was a clerk for the postal service. One of his favorite jobs was working the window and serving customers—selling stamps, weighing parcels and such. He liked doing the school field trips when kids would come and tour the post office, and he always had lollipops to hand out.

One day an irate customer stormed up to the service window.

"Why ain't y'all found me yet?" she yelled. "I need my check!"

My dad told her to calm down and explain the problem. Seems the lady went from Mississippi to Chicago, Illinois every summer to babysit her sister's children. And her mail followed her. Dad asked her the date she had filled out the official change of address.

"I never did before!" she shouted at him. "Y'all just always found me. It's your job to know where everyone lives."

My dad tried to explain that no, the post office didn't keep track of people. If someone moved and wanted their mail forwarded to the new address, they had to fill out a form that authorizes the post office to send the mail from the old address to the new.

Someone must have turned in the COA (change of address) for her in the past but had forgotten this time. The lady filled out the form under protest.

"Y'all always found me before!"

Unwelcome

I have delivered mail to many addresses. I started my career as a sub on route 13 but soon trained on routes 15, 16, 4, 14, and 17. Five routes moved to an adjacent town when it built its own post office. In the years that followed, my office grew until we replaced those five routes and gained eight more. I went full-time and ran routes 14, 17, 2, 15 and route 1. In all, I can say I've delivered over 500 miles of routes in the city where I work. And thousands and thousands of addresses.

Among my customers are a lot of churches. Big churches with lots of buildings and little churches with grass parking lots. And many denominations, although mostly Christian. I love churches on my route. They get a lot of mail so that's job security. The secretaries are nice and the bathrooms are clean. When the weather is dangerous, I know I can go to the nearest church for shelter.

My experience with the churches on my routes

has been overwhelmingly positive. Except once.

Churches have youth groups. Youth groups have fundraisers. A church on my route many years ago was having a BBQ chicken dinner and a car wash to raise money for a youth mission. I was running early and decided to get my truck washed and have a meal while I waited. The chicken smelled great as I pulled into the parking lot. When I got out of my truck, a very large man walked up to me. The man was not friendly. I told him I was there to get a dinner and my truck washed to support the kids. "No," he told me, "We don't want your business."

I just stared at him. "I'm the mail carrier for this area."

"I don't care," he said. "Leave."

His reason had nothing to do with the post office. If I told you what I thought that reason was you wouldn't believe me.

He was a lot bigger than I am and I was obviously unwelcome. I left.

Don't Ask

Some days a rural letter carrier is rushing to meet the dispatch truck. Other days we can go more slowly and appreciate the flowers. It depends on several factors.

Rural mail carriers work on salary. Periodically, the post office "counts" the mail and results are calculated by a confusing formula into how many hours on average it takes each route to run each day. And that's what we get paid. If we work fewer hours (less mail) one day, we still get paid for the same amount of hours. If we work more hours (usually), we still get paid only for those hours from the count.

Mail carriers are human. I have kids and horses. Some days I need to rush home for ball games, dance recitals, sickness and other life events. So I have learned that when I'm in a hurry, there are some things to never ask a customer.

The first one is, "How are you feeling today?"

Because the answer can be a lengthy recitation of health matters up to and including birth—either their own or those of everyone in their family, with all the gory bits.

Another is, "How can I help you?" Because of these fateful words, carriers have: changed light bulbs and tires, written checks out for the legally blind, picked garden vegetables, mowed lawns, fed dogs for vacationers, and shucked corn.

And don't ask, on observing their beloved pet, "What kind of dog is that?" The result is a pedigree (weather the animal is registered or not). From this I've learned the life histories of many a mongrel. And that a six-foot chain link fence will not keep out a determined Doberman or Labrador that is intent on becoming a father.

Trespassing

For the most part, my job as a rural letter carrier is solitary. I work a few hours inside the post office preparing and organizing the letters, magazines and parcels into what we call the "line of travel." My coworkers are busy with their routes and while we might talk with the people beside us, we keep our hands moving. We hurry to get to the main part of our jobs, delivering the mail.

On the route I see few people. Most of my customers work during the day and the ones who work at night sleep in the daytime. Occasionally, I'll see someone in his or her yard and we wave. Some days I only see customers when I have a piece of mail that requires a signature. So it is a mostly solitary day spent in thoughts about my next delivery, what I have to do when I get off work, what to cook for supper, etc. I'm in my own world mentally.

When a parcel is too large for a mailbox I will

take it to the door and, if it's safe from weather, I leave it. I had a large parcel for an address where I knew no one would be home and I was walking up the sidewalk with the bulky parcel. I was thinking about my kids' schedules (ball practice, homework) and that I needed to stop by the grocery store on the way home. The very loud stern voice caught me completely by surprise. It yelled, "YOU ARE TRESPASSING!" I almost had a heart attack. I had thought I was alone in the world.

I was still alone in the world, I realized, as the voice repeated from a speaker in the door. The recording was motion-activated and I had triggered it when I put the parcel by the door.

CHRISTMAS GIFTS

Someone recently asked me what my favorite Christmas gift from a mail customer was. I had skipped a couple of meals that day so my first thought was about food.

Over the years I have received some yummy presents. Some of the most memorable are hot chocolate and warm banana nut bread on a cold icy day, smoked ham, cookies, divinity (my favorite!), frozen Snickers bars and ice water on a hot day and more cookies. Christmas cards and nice notes are always appreciated and brighten my day.

This is my favorite Christmas gift. I received an ordinary glass ornament with wiggly writing that said #1 Mail Carrier. I gave the customer a thank-you note and put the ornament on my tree. The next year, I was personally handed my ornament by the now-first grader. The writing wasn't so wiggly and again proclaimed me #1 Mail Carrier. The third year, the ornament said #1 Mail Lady! As the years went by, the ornaments got more decorative with glitter and stickers.

I still have most of those inexpensive glass ornaments. They are precious to me.

THE NAKED TRUTH TWO

When I first started as a mail carrier, my coworkers filled my ears with unbelievable stories. Dogs climbing in the windows, naked people answering the door, invites for big country lunches and many more. Over thirty years, all of that has happened. And more.

My second naked mail customer was an elderly man. He lived at the end of a long driveway and his was the only house in sight. I had a parcel for him and beeped the horn to let him know I was there. He was walking around the corner of his house as I was getting out of my truck. I jumped back in the truck! He didn't have a stitch of clothing on.

He was very matter of fact. It was "too hot for clothes." I had him sign for the parcel, carefully keeping my eyes on his face. Then I drove to the next house on my route.

His son laughed when I told him. "Dad did it again!"

Well, it *was* really hot that day.

--

CHRISTMAS STAMPS

Rural letter carriers are full-service postal employees. We are considered post offices on wheels. We can mail parcels, get money orders, collect outgoing mail and sell stamps. Except for during the month of December, we will even put the purchased stamps on the outgoing letters for the customers.

December is a very hectic month for the post office with extra catalogs, letter mail, and parcels. It is the only time rural carriers are eligible for overtime. During December, we are not supposed to put stamps on outgoing letters because it is too time-consuming. I will if it's only a few, but I cannot take the time to stamp hundreds.

One Christmas season, I had a customer's daughter visiting her parents for the holidays. She was about my age and was in college in a different state. The daughter met me at the mailbox with a handful of cards and her dad's stamp order. We use bright orange oversized envelopes for stamp purchases and her dad usually ordered a roll, which is a hundred stamps. Was she too late, she asked me, for her Christmas cards to get to her friends before Christmas?

Only if they went out today, I told her. She asked me if I would affix the stamps from her dad's order that day, instead of waiting until the next day. I was running a little early so I said I would. After filling the order from the window clerk, I used part of the roll to put stamps on the daughter's 23 Christmas cards and put them in the outgoing mail. I added the time it took me to do it to my lunchtime so I wouldn't get fussed at by the supervisor.

I guess it was a couple weeks before the dad needed a stamp and that's when he discovered that he didn't have an entire roll. He called the post office and accused me of stealing his stamps. He was a lawyer and a close friend of the state senator's and, by damn, he was going to get me fired. I was a no-good thief and a liar and I wasn't to be trusted with people's mail. The man ranted quite a while, my supervisor told me.

I explained what had happened and my supervisor called the man back and told him his daughter had used the stamps. Again the man cursed me (the phone was on speaker) and said he was going to make sure I was fired. My supervisor asked the man to check with the daughter before filing an official complaint.

The complaint was never filed so I guess the daughter told him I used the stamps on her mail. And he never apologized to me.

THE MURDER OF FLOWERS

One of the fun parts of being a rural letter carrier is the scenery. I love being outdoors, even in all kinds of weather. I get to see the seasons change, the crops grow, the new calves in the pastures and the magnificent tempest of the storms. I watch as my customers' landscapes bloom with the seasons.

The best yard on my route was full of daylilies of all colors and sizes, hydrangeas in white and pink, gardenias and roses, black-eyed susans and orange cosmos and many, many more flowers that I couldn't name. Every day, it was a joy to see this beautiful yard. The owner was a very elderly lady and she loved working in her garden.

She would be out there wearing her old-timey dress and a bonnet to protect her face from the sun.

I worried that one day I would see my customer collapsed in her yard so I would slow down and look closely in the rows of flowers. When I told her my worry, she just laughed and said that would be a good way to go, among the flowers that she loved. Her mind was still sharp at almost 90 years young and she remembered how each precious plant had come into her life: gifts from her husband and children, neighbors and friends. She gave me some daylilies and told me not to thank her, for that would jinx the plants and they might die.

In the fullness of time, the elderly customer could no longer live alone and she moved from my route and my life. I had to watch as each pass by her vacant house showed the neglect of her beloved flowers. I cringed as the daylilies were mowed down.

Years later someone, bought the old house. They ruthlessly ripped out the roses and gardenias, and cut down the wisteria. I had not seen my customer for many years at this point. I was glad she never saw the murder of her flowers.

MAIL FROM JAIL

One of the myths about mail carriers is that we read all the post cards. This is simply not true. We handle thousands of pieces of mail every day and our focus is getting done with the route before the dispatch truck leaves. This is the truck that takes the incoming mail that we picked up that day and moves it along. Missing the dispatch truck is a postal no-no and there are consequences.

If a post card had only a few words, written large and close to the address, we might read them but wouldn't really pay attention. It's all about the address. My mind is on doing my job and getting home. Baseball and dance practice, homework and housework. Life.

Sometimes though, a word will catch the eye and we do pay attention. For me that word was "hate." It was written next to the delivery address and was part of a short sentence: "I HATE you!" I glanced up at the return address. The county jail.

My only option was to deliver the letter. And it wasn't the last.

Over the course of weeks and months, this guy sent thick envelopes to my customer on a regular basis. And as bulky as his letters were, he always added an extra message on the envelope right next to the address.

This is how it progressed:

"I HATE you!" was the first I noticed.

"You made me do it."

"My counselor said it's my fault."

"SORRY I hurt you."

"Miss you and LOVE you."

"ANSWER me damn it!"

"Sorry, sorry, sorry."

"Lawyer says I'm getting out soon!"

"One more week!"

I was not surprised to get a handwritten note in the mailbox informing me that the customer was moving and would not be filing a change of address.

ROLLED

I'm lucky to have schools on my route. They get a lot of mail, which I think of as job security. I also have teachers on my route. And at certain times of year the students participate in a generational tradition.

Many seniors only have a half-day of school. The student parking lot empties and the closest convenience store fills up. The store sells a lot of pizza and soda. And toilet paper.

One of the teachers lives on my route. I serve her mailbox and then turn left and serve a small community, and then turn back on the main road in front of the teacher's house. It takes me only about ten minutes from when I first see her house and then back again.

I served the teacher's box and smiled to see her perfect yard. Grass neat and trimmed, trees and shrubs a healthy green, flowerbeds mulched and watered. Ten minutes later, I stared in shock at her house. Not a person or car was in sight but her house and yard had been transformed. It looked as if it had snowed in her yard. Trees and bushes, chairs and porch rails, and even the mailbox where covered in white... toilet paper. Rolls and rolls and rolls of toilet paper.

I can only guess how many kids it took to do that extensive of a job in so short a time.

No Good Deed... Again

Mail carriers care about our customers. We get to know some better than others as the years go by. The most common way a carrier rescues a customer is by noticing that the mail hasn't been picked up. Almost every coworker I know has taken the extra time to check on someone. I've done this many times in my 30-plus years.

Once, a customer had not picked up her mail because had a small stroke. She was slightly confused and couldn't talk clearly. She gave me her address book and pointed to a name. I called the number, her daughter's, and explained that Mrs. M was not acting normally. I waited with her until the ambulance arrived. She kept patting my hand as if to reassure me.

Another time I was driving by a house when I heard a car horn beeping. It was a short, dead-end road that I turned around and served the mailboxes on the way back. The car horn wasn't beeping when

I came back but instead of putting the mail in the box, I drove up to the house. Mrs. D was lying on the ground in her carport, her wheelchair overturned.

I jumped out and ran to her. She was sobbing and had scrapes and bruises. She wanted me to help her up but I was afraid to move her. Her son-in-law lived up the road so I drove there and brought him back. We got Mrs. D back in her wheelchair and in her house. She had fallen on her way to her car. She had the presence of mind to use her alarm on the keys to get attention. It was over a hundred degrees that day and I shudder to think what might have happened.

A few days later, I stopped in to see how Mrs. D was doing. While I didn't expect appreciation, I wasn't prepared for her first words. I asked how she was feeling and her reply was an abrupt "Fine." Then she proceeded to complain loudly and in detail about the stamps I've been selling her. She was sick and tired of flag stamps and those ugly vegetable stamps.

The farmers' market forever stamps are my personal favorites.

Best U.S.P.S. Customers!

If being a good mail carrier means liking your job, then I am a great mail lady. I love my route. It is more than 70 miles long, which is job security without being overlong. I have some areas with mailboxes close together and some areas are spread out. There are a couple of hills where I can stop and see for miles over forest and field. I have schools and churches, small country stores and businesses run out of garages.

And I have the best customers ever. I get smiles and waves as I serve the mailboxes, cards and sweet treats for Christmas. I've received generous garden produce and help with flat tires. During the postal food drive every May, my customers fill my truck with donations for the local food banks.

I am truly blessed.

SECRET SWEET CORN

Sometimes when I meet a customer on my route, we strike up a conversation. It could be about the mail, children, grandkids, beloved dogs, health, weather or gardens. Sometimes it's a combination.

When I hadn't seen one of my favorite customers for a while, I asked her daughter how things were going. Not good, I learned. Mom had health problems and was losing her mobility. I know she loved her vegetable garden so I asked how it was doing. The daughter told me the kids kept up most of the veggies but they had given up on the corn. It was sad because their momma really liked sweet corn. My dad loves his corn, too, I told her and went on with my route.

Weeks later, my dad's corn came in and it was a bumper crop. Corn everywhere and not even the deer, raccoons, birds, family, coworkers and neighbors could use it all. I remembered my customer who loved corn and my dad and I picked her almost a hundred ears.

The next morning, I took the sacks and two buckets and left the corn in her carport. It was before work and really early so I didn't wake them. I laughed to myself thinking how surprised they would be and decided not to tell them it was I (although I wouldn't have minded getting my buckets back).

No worries. Later that day when I approached their mailbox, my buckets where hanging from the mailbox post. Inside the box was a sweet thank you note for the corn.

I guess my secret sweet corn wasn't so secret after all.

SURPRISED DELIVERY

I have three children, two grandchildren and one ex-husband. As the kids were growing up, I would tell them the funny things that happened to me. I was a 4H youth leader for more than ten years and had three groups; these kids also liked my mail carrier stories.

My adult children introduced me to Facebook and I used it to check up on them. Then when I was going through a difficult personal event, I decided to post my mail carrier stories and concentrate on the humorous side of life. Friends and family liked them and I had lots of people asking to be added to my page. I admit it was an ego booster when I was feeling low.

Then someone commented that I should put the stories in a book. I was surprised when I counted and realized how many I had. So *The Laughing Postman* was written and published as an eBook on Amazon. Fun! Many more stories later, I added another eBook called *The Laughing Postman Delivers.* Requests for a print book led me to combine the two eBooks into a printed book.

For legal (divorce) reasons I hadn't advertised my books. News spread on Facebook and by word of mouth. People would see me in the store and ask for a copy. My relatives were very supportive. My son and son-in-law made the books available at their businesses.

The event that made me feel like a real author happened on my mail route. I delivered an Amazon parcel to a favorite customer. She asked me to wait just a moment and she opened her parcel. She showed me her copy of my book and asked me to sign it. I smiled for days and smile again whenever I think of it.

TO MY READERS

I hope you've enjoyed *The Laughing Postman Redelivers*. I'd love to hear from you! My email address is thelaughingpostman@gmail.com. I welcome comments and hope you will leave a review on Amazon.

A special thanks to my Facebook friends for all the comments and "likes." I post my stories on the Facebook group page: The Laughing Postman.

Made in the USA
San Bernardino, CA
30 July 2016